PTSD

How to Overcome Trauma and Dissociative Disorders

(Therapeutic Treatment Guide of Anxiety and Ptsd)

Jeanette Pearson

Published by Tomas Edwards

© **Jeanette Pearson**

All Rights Reserved

Ptsd: How to Overcome Trauma and Dissociative Disorders
(Therapeutic Treatment Guide of Anxiety and Ptsd)

ISBN 978-1-990268-53-3

All rights reserved. No part of this guide may be reproduced in any form without permission in writing from the publisher except in the case of brief quotations embodied in critical articles or reviews.

Legal & Disclaimer

The information contained in this book is not designed to replace or take the place of any form of medicine or professional medical advice. The information in this book has been provided for educational and entertainment purposes only.

The information contained in this book has been compiled from sources deemed reliable, and it is accurate to the best of the Author's knowledge; however, the Author cannot guarantee its accuracy and validity and cannot be held liable for any errors or omissions. Changes are periodically made to this book. You must consult your doctor or get professional medical advice before using any of the suggested remedies, techniques, or information in this book.

Upon using the information contained in this book, you agree to hold harmless the Author from and against any damages, costs, and expenses, including any legal fees potentially resulting from the application of any of the information provided by this guide. This disclaimer applies to any damages or injury caused by the use and application, whether directly or indirectly, of any advice or information presented, whether for breach of contract, tort, negligence, personal injury, criminal intent, or under any other cause of action.

You agree to accept all risks of using the information presented inside this book. You need to consult a professional medical practitioner in order to ensure you are both able and healthy enough to participate in this program.

Table of Contents

INTRODUCTION 1

CHAPTER 1: LIFE BEYOND LABELS: COMPLEX PTSD AND ITS TYPICAL SOURCES 5

CHAPTER 2: WHAT TO DO TO HEAL 27

CHAPTER 3: MANAGING STRESS - THE BASICS 37

CHAPTER 4: CONDITIONING OF THE MIND 57

CHAPTER 5: LEVELS OF RECOVERING 61

CHAPTER 6: WHO GETS PTSD? 89

CHAPTER 7: DIAGNOSIS 99

CHAPTER 8: MASSAGE FOR PTSD 104

CONCLUSION 118

Introduction

Post Traumatic Stress Disorder, or PTSD, is a condition that is as old as mankind itself. The only difference between then and now is that first, people didn't know that there was such a thing and second, it has become more of an epidemic than a mere disorder.

PTSD, however, is indeed real, and it troubles many people each year. It's almost impossible to crunch the numbers because plenty of people out there don't even know that they have it. Even then, it's still safe to say that there are millions of people who are experiencing PTSD, many of which life with, and sadly, die with PTSD undiagnosed.

People who live with PTSD don't just live less fulfilling lives, but they tend to make life more difficult for those around them as well. And because PTSD can affect anyone — parents, children, friends, and loved ones — this condition has the potential to wreck, or at least cripple, entire communities from reaching their potentials.

Yes, PTSD can affect anyone. While the scenario of an army veteran experiencing PTSD in his retirement years is an all too common one, it's important to know that regular individuals can develop the condition just as easily through experiences that can equal the trauma of being in a war. This goes beyond the effects of calamities like earthquakes and hurricanes or terrible experiences like crime. Literally anyone can experience something that traumatizes them to the point of developing PTSD.

The sad reality is, however, that many people go through their lives not knowing they have it. And even if they do know they have it, they don't know there is a way to overcome the disorder. Yet many of those who do know about the condition, and realize that treatment options are available, still choose to procrastinate in getting help, for one reason or another.

This is where you and this book come into play. Despite the facts stated above, the most important thing to remember is that PTSD can indeed be treated, and it starts with a friend or family member that recognizes their loved one may be suffering. Keep in mind, much like any other condition or illness, chances are that your loved one – the person in the midst of PTSD resulting from a traumatic experience – is unable to work things out on their own. They need you to help.

Perhaps you think of PTSD as a complex scientific concept that only psychologists should meddle with. Well, that's partially true, but it's partially not. It is most definitely something that everyone should be aware of because there are plenty of ways you can help. This book is geared towards simplifying PTSD for you, and explaining what your role can be in helping your loved one recover. The solution to PTSD rests in knowing how to identify it in others (or perhaps even in yourself), and how to give them the support and understanding they need to make a full recovery. That's exactly what this ebook is designed to help you do. So don't wait any longer: Be proactive in helping to save your loved one - and those around him - from being deprived of a better life. Read on to learn more.

Chapter 1: Life Beyond Labels: Complex Ptsd And Its Typical Sources

As so aptly echoed in Stephen King's quote about hell, I strongly concur how this "blue and lonely section of hell" connotation, with merely a survival mentality of "no maps of the change," depicts the perfect definition to describe my own life experiences with PTSD. I always felt like my peers lived a perfect life, while I sat alone on the side lines, just faking happiness and normal. Have you also felt the same when coping with PTSD? I always felt like a fugitive as I harbored such dark secrets in my life for decades.

In sum, Chapter 1 will focus on how to learn, live, and love your life beyond labels much more holistically, peacefully, healthily, and mindfully. I will introduce what complex PTSD really means, what it entails, how research describes it, and also its typical sources and origins in this section.

Word Up Ice Breaker

Words are so powerful as they set the tone for our mindset, emotions, attitudes, and actions. Start with this basic ice breaker that enables us to find our voices again after the trauma that we have encountered. Try this brief exercise. How would you articulate your PTSD in one word? Jot down or draw the first word that appears in your mind: _____. Since the past is behind us, I want to guide you to take back your power right now.

Next, envision how you can use your chosen word to label your past, but not allow it to define your present. It is all about living in the NOW! This type of transformative exercise is exactly what this workbook seeks to accomplish by changing your thoughts more mindfully. One of the best motivators for me is to recognize how without the murky mud and filthy dirt, a gorgeous lotus flower could never bloom without the darkness to nurture it. By finding ways to show that we can still thrive and bloom amid the ugliness of our pasts, we can walk more mindfully toward healing. What metaphor can you utilize to ensure that your life can still blossom despite complex PTSD experiences?

Word Up 2 Exercise

Words are, of course, the most powerful drug used by mankind." — Rudyard Kipling

Now choose one word to describe your present situation with PTSD recovery. Record or draw your word here and make it motivational:

_____
_____

My examples are Resilient and Thriving. I choose it because I do not merely want to survive and walk through the daily motions of life; instead, I aim to thrive and shine despite the paralysis that complex PTSD can inflict upon me!

Do you ever wish that you could hit rewind or pause to alter the events in your lifetime? Unfortunately, we do not have access to any advanced time machine or radical remote control that can change our pasts, but we all possess the power to change how we move past it and grow accordingly.

As a result, resilience is one of the most paramount goals and recurrent themes in this workbook. Self-growth and self-awareness are the two ingredients that I also urge you to use, like a master chef from one of those intense TV cooking competitions. Let us beat PTSD the way we try to grill and chill over Bobby Flay and Rachael Ray with our culinary creations! Apply your own sheer willpower, lessons, free will, tenacity, and fortitude from this workbook to live beyond the labels of complex PTSD today!

Started from the Bottom Exercise

"I like good strong words that mean something..."
— Louisa May Alcott, Little Women

Like Drake's clever and catchy song with the same title, take a few minutes, close your eyes, and recall your lowest point with PTSD. I then encourage you to take a moment and complete this sentence starter, "From _____ to _____" as you re-write your lowest point to show your ability to gain resilience through goal setting to the present. Once you record your goals, you will likely sense an eminent shift.

For example, I recorded from "From hell to healed" or from "From hell to healthy." Strive to set at least 5 goals that you hope to achieve from this book in this exercise:

1.

_____

_____

2.

_____

_____

3.

_____

_____

4.

_____

_____

5.

_____

_____

In other words, mindfulness practitioners call this type of exercise "setting your intentions" Are you ready to set your personal and earnest intentions to transform holistically from labels to live your best life from now on? I love to use the ladder metaphor to inspire my own climb or ability to transcend the traumas of my past. What metaphor will you personally employ to inspire you along the

way? Draw or list it here:
_____

From Hell to Healing: What Is PTSD?

"What is hell? I maintain that it is the suffering of being unable to love."
— Fyodor Dostoevsky, The Brothers Karamazov

Despite the literary, fictitious nature of Dostoevsky's writings in this preceding quote, "hell" certainly seems like the most concise and accurate way to encompass the multiple layers of impacts that linger from complex PTSD in any form. Before we examine the all-encompassing ramifications that complex PTSD tend to inflict upon us, I first want to define what complex PTSD truly is, since it is a term that is often thrown around haphazardly, often without proper understanding of its various parts and effects. In the process, I want to dispel any mainstream myths, stigmas, or stereotypes that often penetrate when we discuss what PTSD really entails.

Again, healing from the hell of PTSD starts in baby steps and emanates directly from our own sense of self-awareness and mindfulness. The critical first baby steps involve the process of addressing and defining exactly what happened to us. Think of this phase as a reality check. For me, I have literally buried so many memories from childhood or have been raised on limitless lies about my past, so this step was a majorly sticky one for me to conquer.

What did I learn from getting "unstuck?" I encourage you to stay open, be honest, go slow, breathe, remain patient, and be strong. Without completing this necessary work, we are going to remain stuck in deep denial and dire detachment for the rest of our lives from complex PTSD.

First of all, how is complex PTSD officially defined? It is short for the significant health and mental health issue called "post-traumatic stress disorder, which may occur after prolonged or repeated traumatic events" (https://www.researchgate.net/publication/318156926_Posttraumatic_Stress_Disorder_and_Emotion-Focused_Coping_Among_Disaster _Mental_Health_Counselors), according to Pow & Cashwell (2017). Miksanek (2019) further unveils in "The Unspeakable Mind: Stories of Trauma and Healing from the Frontlines of PTSD Science" from Booklist how it reflects "a challenging condition with a collection of possible symptoms— nightmares, relentless harmful emotions (anger, fear, guilt), hypervigilance, flashbacks, and an amplified startle response" (p. 11). We often hear about flight or fight tendencies, which are frequently some of the main features of complex PSTD. While these are true, the notion that PTSD can only happen in wartime or to military members is false. Of course military members experience PTSD are high rates due to the vicious nature of war and combat exposure, this workbook aims to alleviate any other myths about complex PTSD through our discovery process.

Be Kind to Rewind Exercise

"Life can only be understood backwards; but it must be lived forwards." — Søren Kierkegaard

Pause for a moment and name the 3 more prevalent symptoms of PTSD that you personally recognize and struggle with the most in your own inner and outer life today:

1._____2. _____3._____.

In my own struggles, here are my top 3:

Perfectionist tendencies

Trying to control everyone and everything since I lacked control when I experienced trauma and victimization.

Eating disorders/disordered eating

Imagine that you have a remote control that can transport you back in time. Then take a few minutes and "rewind." Identify when these signs first likely appeared. Was it after your divorce? A few months after your cousin was killed in that horrific, senseless act of violence? Did it happen every night when you went to bed fearing another sexual assault from a step-parent as a young child?

While this exercise is certainly not the easiest as far as its likelihood to trigger some heavy emotional memories and feelings, it is vital work for us to put all the pieces of our journey into PTSD into logical perspective by addressing the past with mindfulness and patience.

Let us know get back to more definition clarity. Contrary to some rampant rumors, menacing myths, and strange stigmas that may insinuate that you can develop PTSD after watching a horror movie or dramatic episode of Judge Judy, experts clarify how it technically results following firsthand exposure to one or more traumatic events and may lead to a wide range of symptoms: "according to the Diagnostic and Statistical Manual of Mental Disorders diagnostic criteria, it is follows the presence of four key indicators: (a) intrusion, (b) avoidance, (c) negative alterations in cognition and mood, and (d) alterations in arousal and reactivity" (https://www.researchgate.net/publicatio n/318156926_Posttraumatic_Stress_Disor der_and_Emotion-Focused_Coping_Among_Disaster _Mental_Health_Counselors).

Along the same lines, timing is also significant when defining PTSD since symptoms. A diagnosis tends to focus on symptoms that persist for more than a month may signal the onset of PTSD, according to the (2011) article called "Warning Signs and Ways to Help" from Newsweek. Similarly, PTSD is also typically distinguished by what I call the "Why Me's?"

Why Me's?

"You cannot continue to victimize someone else just because you yourself were a victim once—there has to be a limit"
— Edward Said

Edward Said's compelling quote offers such valid advice about falling prey to a victim mentality and approach after one experiences complex PTSD. The cycle of PTSD, though, can be broken. Stop victimizing others because you were hurt and quit hurting yourself. Instead, review my list and see if you find yourself operating from this sort of blame game position or reactionary stance in your own life:

W is for **Withdrawal:** Are you depressed, abstaining from activities that you once loved, isolating yourself, devoid of friends and solid work relationships? Are you estranged from loved ones and family members?

H is for **Hypervigilance:** Does your nervous system always seem to be in overdrive? Do you reside in a perpetual state of flight or fight?

Y is for **You're** on Always Edge: Do you exhibit jumpy, testy, or erratic behaviors and responses to others at work, in friendships, relationships, or online postings?

M is for **Memories** That Haunt: Are you suffering from sleep problems, flashbacks, and/or recurrent dreams that terrorize and re-visit the initial trauma repeatedly?

E is for **Engaging** in **Extra** Vigilance: Do you often notice yourself as being verbally, emotionally, psychological, or physically reactive or "testy" to people, events, sounds, smells, and other triggers?

S is for **Suffering** in **Silence**: Have you repressed your traumas? Do you resist the urge to talk or write about it with others or even yourself?

Why Me? Exercise

After carefully reviewing the list above, reflect honestly on the Why Me's? Next, circle all of the ones that are presently holding you back from living your best, healthiest, and happiest life right now. Then star the top 2-3 that you hope to address first and prioritize after reading this book. Transform from "Why Me" to becoming free! You can also use this time to journal or write about any feelings that emerge during this exercise. Drawing is also a great way to release those emotions, too:

Other Sources of Complex PTSD

"What sticks to memory, often, are those odd little fragments that have no beginning and no end..."
— Tim O'Brien, The Things They Carried

Now that you know the basic definitions and underlying components of what PTSD entails, I want to discuss other sources. As mentioned earlier, complex PTSD is often associated strictly to military members and veterans, but it is also possible for children, teens, and all civilians to also develop it. In my case, I likely suffered from it since childhood but did not receive an official diagnosis until later in life because I did not receive therapy or counseling until my college years.

As far as military statistics, PTSD refers to one of the most common and severe mental health conditions diagnosed among military at an average rate of up "to 30% of veterans from Operation Iraqi Freedom/Operation Enduring Freedom (OIF/OEF)"
(https://www.ncbi.nlm.nih.gov/pubmed/2

7152480). It is found in both men and women who serve as well as all lifestyles, sexual orientations, ranks, ages, demographics, etc.

To give some personal insights from my own past, my dad, grandfather, and uncles were all exposed to war trauma in the days before an official PTSD diagnosis. They were "shell-shocked," as the term mostly characterized from the past. Both served in deadly combat but never received help because they lived in times and places where "real men" did not talk about their emotions.

While I never went to a physical war, I saw daily battles during my childhood and adolescent years in rural Appalachia. I saw beatings, chokings, weapons pulled, and threats. I also followed in their silent footsteps and never talked to friends, coaches, teachers, or school counselors about any of my trauma until I entered college.

In sum, our PTSD battles scars are not always physical in nature. Kumari & Mukhopadhyay (2016) further dispel myths that complex PTSD can only arise from war or physical trauma; instead, they firmly suggest how it "can be caused by an overwhelmingly negative event that causes a lasting impact on the victim's mental and emotional stability. Many sources of trauma are physically violent in nature, while others are psychological" (p. 1036). Sometimes the line that divides the sources is so fine, as there are usually so many overlaps, crisscrosses, and "interlocking spider webs," as I like to think of them, right?

Diagramming "Danger Activity

The past is never where you think you left it."
— Katherine Anne Porter

As you trace the roots of your own path with PTSD, diagram some of the likely sources here in this space:

Additionally, in a comprehensive article called "Shell Shocking Impacts from PTSD" by Getz, Carandang, Harpenau, & Holt (2017), the writers further explain how complex PTSD is a mental health condition that develops after a life-threatening event and seems to impact more women than men as "approximately 10% of women develop PTSD sometime in their lives compared to 4% of men" (p. 36) . Again, PTSD, like so many other challenges, does not discriminate and can impact all ages, lifestyles, genders, political affiliations, sexual orientation, religions, cultures, socioeconomic statuses, abilities, disabilities, backgrounds, etc.

Likewise, other common sources, besides military service, wartime, and combat exposure, may also result from the following examples:

Mass shootings, school shootings, and terror attacks

Rape, incest, domestic violence, IPV, child abuse, accidents, and fires (Miksanek, 2019, p. 11).

Gang violence, involvement or victimization from acts of crime

Homelessness, victims of human trafficking, kidnapping, etc.

Refugee status, living amid wars and political persecutions, and immigration experiences

Aftermath from natural disasters like earthquakes, typhoons, hurricanes, wildfires, tornadoes, etc.

Cases of racial profiling and victims from hate crimes

Parents' divorces, motor vehicle accidents, serious illnesses or deaths of family members, and moves to new places (Webb, 2011).

Since scholars are still trying to discern why some people are more susceptible to

PTSD than others, it is imperative to reiterate that trauma can impact people in different ways. Dr. William Copeland, an associate professor in the psychiatry department at Duke University in Durham, N.C., breaks it down by commenting how "What's traumatic for one person might be different from what's traumatic for someone else," he notes. Some doctors think that it is more important to focus on a person's response rather than the event that caused it" (Webb, 2011, p. 11). I am not Dr. Freud by any means, but I would like to add lack of response to it since repression and denial can also play big parts in PTSD.

Take my own upbringing case of family feuds and dysfunctional domestic dramas, for example. My brother and I were only two years apart, so we both witnessed the same violence and abuse instances in our household. However, we each reacted to and processed these events so differently. I initially developed an eating disorder as a teen to try and control the uncontrollable events and evils within my life; he, on the other hand, sadly followed in my father's abusive footsteps and exhibited the same levels of dating violence and physical abuse to his teen girlfriends and other women through several marriages into adulthood that ended in divorce, anxiety, mental problems, job-related dysfunction, depression, and the perpetual PTSD!

Chapter 2: What To Do To Heal

Passionate injury is all over the place, thus a considerable lot of us are influenced by it.

At the point when we lose a person or thing we love, or an unpleasant occasion breaks separated our feeling that all is well with the world, we can start to see our condition and people around us as risky. Regardless of whether a specific occasion doesn't cause us any physical mischief, being in a condition of dread can in any case cause us to become damaged. Before we get into the 5 stages of mending from enthusiastic injury, we should investigate basic structures and side effects that frequently go with it.

Basic kinds of passionate injury:

- Divorce or relationship separation

- Loss of wellbeing

- Losing an employment
- Loss of budgetary security
- Miscarriage
- Retirement
- Death of a pet
- Loss of an appreciated dream
- A friend or family member's not kidding disease
- Loss of a fellowship
- Loss of security after an injury
- Selling the family home

Because of enthusiastic injury, we start to feel numb, separated and lose our trust in others. It can require some investment for this torment to leave, and for us to have a sense of security once more. On the off chance that the injury we've encountered is mental, we may experience the ill effects of disturbing recollections, uneasiness and feelings.

Injury makes a stun our brains, bodies and spirits, which can prompt passionate issues later on. There are subjective, conduct, physical, and mental responses to passionate injury.

Here are probably the most well-known passionate reactions:

- Increased excitement

- Post horrendous pressure issue

- Avoidance of social settings, companions, friends and family

- Feelings of outrage or crabbiness, sensitivity

- Sense of blame and disgrace

- Grief and discouragement

- Self-picture and perspectives on the world become progressively pessimistic

- Sexual connections endure

- Drug and liquor misuse

The passionate reactions recorded above can make us feel as if we're going insane or "losing it". Have you at any point seen that, following a horrible accident, your physical wellbeing starts to show side effects?

Regardless of whether the injury caused direct physical damage, or the substantial vitality of torment and negative feeling wore you out, the two conditions are joined by profound enthusiastic torment which can make you sick. Sleep deprivation, bad dreams, interminable exhaustion, trouble concentrating, alarm assaults, restlessness, unsettling, muscle strain and a quick heartbeat are for the most part physical side effects of passionate pressure.

Untreated passionate injury additionally has genuine symptoms.

In the event that unaddressed and left untreated, passionate injury can result in:

• Self-damaging and indiscreet practices

- Uncontrollable responsive contemplations

- Feelings of disgrace, blame, sadness, or gloom

- Loss of previous conviction frameworks

- Compulsive social issues

- Substance use difficulties

- Sexual issues

- Inability to keep up cozy connections or keep up fitting companionships

- Hostility and contentiousness

- Introversion

- Feelings of being undermined

At the point when we experience passionate injury, frequently, we're advised to concentrate on ourselves— however that can be a lot more difficult than one might expect. At the point when it feels like the heaviness of the world is on your shoulders, it's trying to try and discover the solidarity to lift your leg, and start placing one foot before the other. Truth be told, discovering solidarity to mend from passionate injury can be absolutely debilitating and weakening now and again—notwithstanding, it's one of the most significant things you can accomplish for your prosperity. It's critical to keep up the guideline of "keeping it straightforward" when you start your recuperating venture, to maintain a strategic distance from overpower, disappointment or the craving to surrender completely. In light of that, here are five straightforward yet important strides for mending:

5 Simple Steps to Healing From Emotional Trauma

1. Be Happy to Heal

The longing to feel better can be your best partner making progress toward recuperation. Try not to yield to the self image, which will attempt to let you know there's a major issue with you: there's nothing amiss with you. The responses you experience in light of injury are just reactions—they are not what your identity is.

2. Acknowledge Support From Loved Ones

When recuperating from enthusiastic injury, it's essential to interface with others routinely and abstain from confining yourself. It takes a town to bring up a youngster, however it likewise takes a town to recuperate an individual. Encircle yourself with the individuals who backing, love and regard you will be priceless on your way to mending.

3. Look for The Assistance of Trained Professionals

You may wish to go to individual or gathering treatment, search out master feelings and get the assistance of somebody prepared in the field of passionate injury, who you feel good with and trust. Medications may concentrate on training, stress the board strategies, the arrival of body recollections, and smothered feelings that are causing physical and mental agony.

4. Practice Meditation and Mindfulness

Contemplation helps calm the jabber of the psyche, to enable you to encounter knowledge, acknowledgment and another thankfulness forever. Enthusiastic injury gets put away inside the body, so notwithstanding treatment sessions, the body extraordinarily profits by entering negligent minutes and having a care practice.

5. Fuse Movement Into Your Daily Routine

Yoga and different types of physical action discharge endorphins, and make you have a sense of security and stable. It's imperative to guarantee you consistently take part in physical action to help make positive sentiments which have been torn down from enthusiastic injury.

It might be difficult to accept this now, however you should recall the heart heals. Love yourself enough to accept that you merit shelter from agony and enduring. With confidence and ability to make the correct strides, you'll experience new degrees of delight, thankfulness, and imperativeness once you've mended.

"In the event that you are to free your heart, you should grasp your excruciating emotions, have confidence that your considerations will emerge and stop of their agreement. They will pass in the event that you can confront them head on, with kind eyes. Your musings and emotions will break up on the off chance that you don't attempt to clutch them or push them away. Thinking will scatter. Trust in this all inclusive law of progress."

— Detox Your Heart: Meditations for Healing Emotional Trauma

T – Trust yourself, family, companions and experts to help you

R – Recovery is a procedure that requires significant investment and persistence

A – Attend to yourself with affection and self-care

U – Understand enthusiastic injury isn't your flaw

M – Meditation, Mindfulness, and Movement are basic for mending

A – Accept that you are an entire individual

Chapter 3: Managing Stress - The Basics

Though stress can wreak havoc on your life, a stress management strategy can seem overwhelming in its own right. Almost always, when I first recommend stress management to people, their first response is that they don't have time, they're too busy, it's too much work, or, most commonly of all, that they've already tried stress management and it didn't work.

But none of these things are true. At least, not if you don't want them to be. If you feel like you don't have the time or you're too busy to manage your stress, don't worry. It's okay to go slow, and go at a pace that works best for you. There are no deadlines in stress management. If you only have 10 minutes a day to spare, that's fine. If you only have 10 minutes a week to spare, that's fine too. The only important thing is to stay committed and put yourself on a regular schedule. Don't tell yourself you'll do it "whenever you have time." If you do that, you'll never get around to it, and give up before you've really even started.

Stress management is a skill, and like all skills, it takes time and practice to learn. You can't master it overnight, no matter how hard you try. So you might as well go slow. Overwhelming yourself will actually increase your stress - the opposite of what stress management is supposed to do. For ideal results, 15 minutes a day is the recommended time to devote to a daily stress management technique (Avoiding Roadblocks to Stress Reduction, 2016). This might sound like a long time, but that 15 minutes can happen during a coffee break, a lunch hour, the moment that you get home from work, or during your morning commute.

If you are resistant to taking on a new project or feel like stress management is simply too much work, just remember that there is no one right way to manage your stress. Everyone's stressors are unique, and everyone's idea of relaxation is different. A beach in the Caribbean might sound like heaven to you, but it might sound like hell to someone else. Don't be afraid to drop or modify a stress management technique if it doesn't work for you. But remember, it may take awhile before many of these techniques start to show results. If you begin to dread your designated 15 minutes of daily meditation, try instead to experiment with different kinds of meditation, or even move on to a different technique entirely.

That being said, try to keep your mind open and give new things a try. Some of these stress reduction techniques might feel a little strange or uncomfortable at first. Some may be familiar to you, while others might be completely new. With increasing amounts of stress in the world, different stress management techniques may have gained mainstream attention.

This is both a good and a bad thing. For example, you may have heard of breathing exercises before, or even tried a few of them yourself. But the context in which you were introduced to this concept can sometimes affect the way that you think about it. Try to have an open mind, and give these techniques an honest try before you rule them out. You might be surprised at what starts to work for you once you find a way to work it comfortably into your daily routine.

Most methods and techniques require practice before you get them completely right. Approach stress management the same way you would approach learning to ride a bike or drive a car. You won't do it perfectly the first time. Or the second. Or even the third. Though stress management can seem like an intellectual pursuit, it's not enough to only read about it. Anyone can understand how to drive a car from a simple explanation. But to get behind the wheel is a different kind of learning. When you try out a stress management technique, you get behind the wheel, so to speak. So be patient, be open, and eventually you will get into a style and rhythm that is comfortable for you.

It is very important to practice stress management techniques in a quiet place. Don't wait until you're in a stressful situation to apply these tactics. Think about it like learning an instrument. You need to practice every single day, so that when the day of the concert arrives, you already know what to do. Stress management keeps your stress levels low all the time, so that when you are faced with a stressful situation, you're able to keep calm and confident. However, a quiet place can be difficult to find if you lead a hectic and busy life, so you might have to settle for places that are less glamorous. If you have your own office, that's a great place to practice undisturbed. If you have your own bedroom, that's another good option. Wherever you choose, try to find a space that's relatively private, where you won't be disturbed by others.

Don't feel the need to embark on this journey alone! If someone else in your life is also dealing with stress and anxiety, ask if they want to practice with you. Many self-care routines, like weight loss or going to the gym, are far more effective when you have someone else to do it with. Stress management is the same. You won't feel as alone or self-conscious if you have someone else to practice with, and you're far more likely to stay committed if you have a friend to cheer you on.

Above all, don't expect overnight results. The stress you're experiencing took years and years to build, and so it may take just as long to completely overcome. That's not meant to scare or discourage you, however. Stress management doesn't have to be an invasive or difficult process, but no matter what, it will be a slow one. Don't get impatient with yourself, and don't be too quick to give up on something that isn't yielding the results you want. Go slow, go easy, and don't be too hard on yourself.

How to Measure Your Stress

How can you measure a feeling? Fortunately for doctors and psychologists, stress isn't just something you **feel**. It also affects your behaviors and your physical wellness. For doctors, stress levels can be easily tracked by looking at physical markers, including blood, urine, and even saliva tests that measure the levels of stress hormones present in your body (Figueroa-Fankhanel, 2014). But stress can also be measured from a psychological perspective. Some methods, like observation and interviews, are conducted by professionals. But there are a number of easy strategies you can employ to measure your stress levels on your own. The following 3-Step Process is a very simple one that will help you check in on your own stress levels. It will help you be more aware of how stress affects you, and help you keep track of your progress as you begin employing techniques for stress management.

Make Yourself a Stress Journal

This can be a physical notebook, a document in your computer, or a dedicated desk drawer. Whatever form it takes, your stress journal is going to be your most important tool as you move forward with your stress management journey. Keeping a record of your stress levels will help you to determine if your stress management techniques are working, and will give you valuable information about yourself that you will need to make the necessary adjustments. Keeping notes in your stress journal does not have to be a difficult task. All you need is 5 minutes a day to update your journal and check in with your emotional and physical wellbeing.

Every day, the first thing you should do when you open your stress journal is rate your stress on a scale from 1-10. This is your gut check, your own personal score. How would you rate your feelings of stress today? If you like, on the first day of every month, take an online PSS test. Pay attention to how your score changes over time. If it's going down, what techniques have you been using that are successful? If it's going up, maybe it's time to change the way you're using your chosen techniques or even try some new techniques altogether.

Once you've recorded your daily score, make a list of any negative physical symptoms you've experienced that day, including pain, fatigue, or other health problems. Finally, write down one word that you would use to describe your mood. Naming your feelings is extremely important for your mental health, but if it's not something you're used to doing, it can sometimes be difficult to find the right words. If you're struggling to describe your emotions accurately, you can find a mood chart online that you can use to help you label your feelings every day.

Recording your stress levels, mood, and physical symptoms every day will give you a lot of information to work with. At the end of your first month, you will be able to look back at your journal and see patterns emerging. You might notice that you usually record having a headache when your stress levels are high. You might notice that you feel irritable all the time, but you only experience anxiety when your stress levels are high. You might find that you were feeling extremely depressed until you started meditating, but once you started that technique, you haven't been feeling so down. Taking just five minutes a day to check in with your feelings can be a stress-reducing technique on its own. Having awareness of how you're feeling and what's going on in your body is perhaps the most important thing you can do when it comes to managing your stress. The unique physical and emotional ways that your body responds to stress is called your "stress signature." Like your fingerprints or your handwriting, your stress signature is unique to you. The more you understand how your body responds to stress, the better you will be at successfully managing it.

Use a Stress Gauge

The most commonly used psychological tool to measure stress levels is called the Perceived Stress Scale, or PSS. If you're someone who likes specificity and you want a more concrete way to measure your stress, there are a number of PSS tests and tools available for free online from reliable websites. This test will give you a number between 0-40 to determine how severe your stress levels are. The test asks you to think about your life over the course of the past month, and so it's most useful when conducted on a monthly basis.

Do a Gut Check

It may seem obvious, but the first step in measuring your stress level is to simply take a step back and ask yourself, "How do I feel?" A gut check is simply giving yourself a second to check in with your body and mind and determine how you're feeling. Remember that stress presents in everyone's body in slightly different ways. If you find yourself feeling stress, take a moment to observe the situation. How would you rate your stress, on a scale from one to ten (one being very low, ten being extremely high)? Think about your physical symptoms. What's happening in your body? Do you feel pain or tension anywhere? Are you experiencing digestive troubles? Are you having trouble performing sexually? Understanding where and how stress is stored in your body will help you to understand just how stressed you are in any given situation. Sometimes we become so used to dealing with stress that we don't even realize how severe our stress is until our body presents with physical symptoms.

Next, observe your mood. Are you feeling depressed? Anxious? Angry? Just as different people's bodies express stress differently, your mind expresses stress in unique ways too. Learning how you emotionally respond to stress is just as important as learning what your physical symptoms are. Some people become extremely depressed when they're under a lot of stress. Other people feel extremely nervous or anxious. The ways that you emotionally respond to stress will give you clues as to what steps are best for you when it comes to managing your stress successfully.

Managing Your Stress - The Three-Step Method

Now that you've checked in, determined your major life stressors and created your stress journal, you're ready to begin taking some real steps to manage your stress levels. The simplest stress management approach is called the Three-Step Method (Manage Your Stress: A Three-Pronged Approach, 2016). Stress management is really about finding a way to manage three different things: your stressors, your thoughts, and your stress responses. Different techniques target different categories, but the best way to manage your stress is to find a balance between all three. Stress management is about finding out how your stressors, your thoughts, and your responses all work together to produce the stress that you feel every day. Only focusing on one or the other will only help you to solve one part of the problem.

The Three-Step Method for Stress Management:

Managing Your Responses

This is where stress management techniques come in. You may not be able to change your stressor, and while positive thinking is always powerful, there are some situations whose silver-linings just aren't bright enough to make a real difference in your stress levels. Techniques like meditation or deep-breathing are techniques that manage the way that your body responds to stress. Meditation won't make your situation disappear, and it may not change your perspective on it. But it will help to reduce the depression or anxiety that you feel in your mind, relieve the physical tension that you feel in your body, and restore your cognitive abilities so that you can continue to work toward solutions. Managing your stress responses often takes the form of lifestyle changes, like exercise or eating healthy. The techniques that you choose can also specifically target your individual responses. For example, if you tend to get headaches when you feel stressed, you might try stretches or breathing exercises that release tension in the neck and shoulders that cause tension headaches. If you experience digestive issues, try to modify your diet to give your gut the extra nutritional support that it needs to keep you happy and healthy in your time of stress.

Manage Your Thoughts

Remember that stress isn't caused by external events. It's caused by how we **perceive** those events. You might find that there are certain stressors that you have very little control over. You can't always avoid being stuck in traffic or an encounter with unpleasant people. But the way that you think about your situation can go a long way to manage your stress. Change the way that you see a stressful situation and sometimes eliminate your stress altogether!

The next time you find yourself in a stressful situation, try to observe your thoughts in the situation. If your thoughts are negative ("Oh my god, what am I going to do? I hate this. I can't believe this is happening…"), then you might need to tackle the way that you think about the stressful situations in your life, especially if they are situations that you can predict. If you hate your long or crowded commute, try to find a way to make it more enjoyable. Make yourself a commute playlist or listen to an audiobook while you sit in traffic. If you have lots of medical appointments, use the time you spend in the waiting room to practice a foreign language or watch an interesting video on YouTube. Whatever the situation may be, try to see what you can gain or learn from it, rather than obsess over how much you hate or dread it. Put all the mental energy that you put into your worry into your enjoyment. At the very least, you can imagine how good you'll feel when the situation is over!

Manage Your Stressors

Often, stress management techniques focus on eliminating or reducing the events, people, or situations that cause you stress in the first place. While this is not always possible, it is still very important to understand where your stress is coming from in the first place. Stressors can be huge life events like divorce or illness, or small inconveniences like a broken shoelace or a crowded subway. The way that you respond to a stressor won't always correspond perfectly to the severity of the stressor itself. If you experience chronic stress, sometimes a small event can trigger a big response.

Earlier in this book, you completed an exercise to determine where the major sources of stress in your life were coming from. Now it's time to go back to those categories. Look at your major stressors and break them down into specific incidents that you can change or modify. For example, if "work" was a major stressor for you, take a moment now to break "work" down into specific examples. What exactly is it about work that stresses you out? Is it your crowded commute? Are you constantly late? Are you generally dissatisfied with your job, company, or department as a career path?

Now that you've made your list, think about how you can turn these "stressors" into "modified stressors." For example, if you have a crowded commute, is it possible to leave the house earlier or later? If you are constantly late for work, determine what makes you late. Do you need to wake up earlier? Do you need to establish better boundaries with the people you live with in the morning? Do you need to arrange for a more reliable mode of transportation?

We are careful to call these "modified stressors" instead of "solutions" because you don't know if they'll work until you try them. Leaving the house 15 minutes earlier than normal might turn your nightmare commute into a dream. But it also might be difficult for you to wake up that early. You might find that your roommate's car blocks you in, or that 15 minutes is not enough time to catch an earlier train. Your solution might solve part of the problem, but it might not completely eliminate your stress. That's okay! Creating a list of modified stressors gives you a better understanding of what you do and don't have control over in your life. It helps you to think creatively about resolving the situations that cause you stress, rather than becoming further and further trapped in feelings of frustration or anxiety. Breaking your stressors down into small, specific situations can also help to make those situations seem more manageable. "Work" is a huge category, with many potential problems and stressors. But "missing deadlines" is a specific problem that can be solved with specific action steps.

Chapter 4: Conditioning Of The Mind

The traditional medical avenues for the treatment of post-traumatic stress disorder include cognitive behavioral therapies. It is recommended to seek the advice of a psychotherapist on the best ways to do that, as well as techniques that you can use yourself at home and do not include medication.

One of the techniques that has produced remarkable positive results is the tapping technique. It can be learned within a weekend of classes and does not need any tools or equipment. It is placed under the general umbrella of an energy psychology method and involves the connection of the emotional issues to the physical ailments.

It uses specific gentle movements with the intent of releasing information stuck somewhere in the human brain, neuro-linguistic programing (otherwise known as

NLP) offering new perspectives as to the quality of life through specific set up phrases and techniques to treat the actual trauma.

The next technique that presented significant reduction of the PTSD symptoms and substance abuse along with general improvement on the emotional numbness, is the transcendental meditation. The technique involves sitting for 15 to 20 minutes twice per day with the eyes closed and repeating a mantra.

Art, music and drama techniques have the purpose of taking the mind off what is bothering it, and help it face the problem. Expressing yourself through drawing, making sculptures, playing some guitar or the piano will transfer the emotions to the hands and to the form of art.

By this transfer to another object, it may be possible for the mind to let go of the ideas and images that it denies to accept and thus acquire the capability to accept the event and move on.

The research on the subject has shown that people that engaged in this form of release needed less medication and with a notion that if the mind is properly stimulated, then it will become stronger and able to deal with the trauma and overcome the physical ailments of PTSD.

The Chinese has created a technique called Qigong. Its purpose is to balance one's "life energy", through alignment of body, breath, meditation and mind for health. It is a technique developed to allow higher levels of awareness, discovery of a person's true nature, and develop one's potential.

The practice comprises of slow flowing motions in conjunction with deep breathing rhythms and the mind in a calm state of meditation. It is considered by the Chinese as most essential for self-healing.

All of the above techniques have the objective of releasing the burden carried in the mind. The deep symptom of the disorder is that the patient cannot accept what happened and move on. Therefore, every attempt should be made to convince your own mind, that whatever happened, happened, it is in the past, and the past cannot be changed. No matter how dire were the consequences of the event that caused the trauma, they belong to the past.

Not accepting the event will not change the fact that the event occurred. You might as well accept the traumatizing event, much in the same way as accepting a bad law from the government.

Chapter 5: Levels Of Recovering

Healing from Complex PTSD is, above all, complex. This is important to emphasize because there are numerous one dimensional approaches to trauma that bill themselves as cure-alls. In my opinion, however, singular approaches are unable to address all the levels of wounding that combine to cause Cptsd.

Moreover, working with simplistic approaches can leave you stranded in toxic shame when you do not achieve the touted results. I was motivated to write this book in large part because of the many times I sank into new levels of self-contempt when the latest panacea therapy did not cure me.

I will use the word "key" repeatedly to describe the various tasks upon which recovering hinges. This book offers a keychain of perspectives and techniques to unlock yourself from being what Alice Miller called a "Prisoner of Childhood."

Abusive and abandoning parents can injure and abandon us on many levels: cognitive, emotional, spiritual, physical and relational. To recover, you need to learn how to support yourself – to meet your unmet developmental needs on each level that is relevant to your experience of childhood trauma.

This chapter is a brief overview of the many tasks involved in Cptsd recovery. These tasks are explored at greater length in Part II. The comprehensive Table of Contents at the beginning of this book will direct you to further information on each of the topics covered in this chapter. Please allow yourself to also use the Table of Contents to explore sections of the book that peak your interest.

Key Developmental Arrests In Cptsd

What follows is a list of some of the most common developmental arrests that occur in Cptsd. You may find that you experience a diminishment or absence of these key features of healthy human being. Typically, survivors will vary on which and how many of these arrests relate to them. Factors affecting this are your 4F type, your childhood abuse/ neglect pattern, your innate nature and any recovery work that you have already accomplished.

Self-acceptance

Clear sense of identity

Self-Compassion

Self-Protection

Capacity to draw comfort from relationship

Ability to relax

Capacity for full self-expression

Willpower & Motivation

Peace of mind

Self-care

Belief that life is a gift

Self-esteem

Self-confidence

My efforts to nurture myself in these arrested areas of development were limited and spoiled in early recovery by a feeling of resentment. "Why do I have to do this?" was a common internal refrain. Resentment that should have been directed toward my parents often boomeranged onto me and spoiled or thwarted my efforts at self-nurturance.

Thankfully ongoing recovery work helped remedy this resentment. It taught me to practice self-care in a spirit of giving to a child who needed and really deserved to be helped.

I find it helpful to approach developmental arrests from the viewpoint of novelist David Mitchell's quip that "...fire is the sun unwinding itself out of the wood". Similarly, effective recovery is unwinding the natural potential you were born with out of your unconscious. This is your innate potential which may be, as yet, unrealized because of your childhood trauma.

An especially tragic developmental arrest that afflicts many survivors is the loss of their will power and self-motivation. Many dysfunctional parents react destructively to their child's budding sense of initiative. If this occurs throughout his childhood, the survivor may feel lost and purposeless in his life. He may drift through his whole life rudderless and without a motor.

Moreover, even when he manages to identify a goal of his own choosing, he may struggle to follow through with extended and concentrated effort. Remedying this developmental arrest is essential because many new psychological studies now show that **persistence** – even more than intelligence or innate talent - is the key psychological characteristic necessary for finding fulfillment in life.

I have worked with many survivors stranded in this form of adult helplessness. Those who recover from it typically do so by engaging extensively in the angering work of grieving that is discussed throughout this book. The ability to invoke willpower seems to be allied to your ability to healthily express your anger. With sufficient recovering, you can learn to manufacture your volition. In the beginning you can fake it until you make it. This is what Stephen Johnson calls "the hard work miracle."

What follows is a concluding comment about development arrests. Some survivors have confidence but not self-esteem. In childhood, my own flight response got channeled into acquiring academic skills for which the outside world rewarded me. But the benefit of these rewards never penetrated my toxic shame enough to allow me to feel that I was a worthwhile person.

My critic, like my parents, always found something flawed in me to contradict the feedback that I was getting. Ninety-nine percent on a test was never a cause for pride. Rather, it was the impetus for a great deal of self-criticism about the missing one percent. Like many other survivors that I have worked with, I developed the **imposter's syndrome**. This syndrome contradicted the outside positive feedback that I was receiving. It insisted that if people really knew me, they would see what a loser I was. Eventually, however, I became confident in my intelligence even though my self-esteem was still abysmal.

COGNITIVE HEALING

The first level of recovery usually involves repairing the damage that Cptsd wreaks on our thoughts and beliefs about ourselves.

Cognitive recovery work aims to make your brain user friendly. It focuses on recognizing and eliminating the destructive thoughts and thinking processes you were indoctrinated with in childhood.

Cognitive healing also depends on learning to choose healthy and more accurate ways of talking to and thinking about yourself. On the broadest level, this involves upgrading the story you tell yourself about your pain.

We need to understand exactly how appalling parenting created the now self-perpetuating trauma that we live in. We can learn to do this in a way that takes the mountain of unfair self-blame off ourselves. We can redirect this blame to our parents' dreadful child-rearing practices. And we can also do this in a way that motivates us to reject their influence so that we can freely orchestrate our journey of recovering.

This work then requires us to build a fierce allegiance to ourselves. Such loyalty strengthens us for the cognitive work of freeing our brains from being conditioned to attack so many normal parts of our selves.

Cognitive work is fundamental to helping you disidentify from the self-hating critic with which your parents inculcated you. As I am writing this, my son's friend synchronistically tells him: "This Lego creature I made spreads brain attack and eats away at the person." I marvel at this synchronicity and think: "What a fitting image for the trauma-inducing parent".

Shrinking The Critic

Early abuse and abandonment forces the child to merge his identity with the superego, the part of the child's brain that learns the rules of his caretakers in order to get and maintain acceptance. However, because acceptance is impossible in the Cptsd-engendering family, the superego gets stuck working overtime to achieve the impossible. Perseverating on finding a formula to win over her parents, the child eventually embraces perfectionism as a strategy to make her parents less dangerous and more engaging. Her one hope is that if she becomes smart, helpful, pretty, and flawless enough, her parents will finally care for her.

Sadly, continued failure at winning their regard forces her to conclude that she is fatally flawed. She is loveless not because of her mistakes, but because she is a mistake. She can only see what is wrong with or missing in her.

Anything she does, says, thinks, imagines or feels has the potential to spiral her down into a depressed abyss of fear and toxic shame. Her superego fledges into a full-blown, trauma-inducing critic.

Self-criticism, then, runs non-stop in a desperate attempt to avoid rejection-inducing mistakes. Drasticizing becomes obsessive to help the child foresee and avoid punishment and worsening abandonment. At the same time, it continuously fills her psyche with stories and images of catastrophe.

The survivor becomes imprisoned by a jailer who will accept nothing but perfection. He is chauffeured by a hysterical driver who sees nothing but danger in every turn of the road. **Chapters 9** and **10** focus extensively on practical tools for shrinking your critic.

The Developmentally Arrested Healthy Ego

Over time the critic becomes more and more synonymous with the survivor's identity. The superego morphs into a totalitarian critic that trumps the development of a healthy ego. [The ego develops later than the superego.]

"Ego", contrary to popular usage, is not a dirty word. In psychology, the term **ego** represents what we typically mean when we use terms like my "self" or my identity. The healthy ego is the user friendly manager of the psyche. Unfortunately,

Cptsd-inducing parents thwart the growth of the ego by undermining the development of the crucial egoic processes of self-compassion and self-protection.

They do this by shaming or intimidating you whenever you have a natural impulse to have sympathy for yourself, or stand up for yourself. The instinct to care for yourself and to protect yourself against unfairness is then forced to become dormant.

Psychoeducation And Cognitive Healing

Becoming psychoeducated about Cptsd is the first level of addressing this poisonous indoctrination of your mind against your healthy ego. When you intricately understand how antagonistic your parents were to your healthy sense of self, you become more motivated to engage in the self-help processes of rectifying their damage. The more you identify their damage the more you know what to fix.

This is essential because without a properly functioning ego, you have no center for making healthy choices and decisions. All too often, your decisions are based on the fear of getting in trouble or getting abandoned, rather than on the principles of having meaningful and equitable interactions with the world.

You can learn to gradually replace the critic's toxic perspective with a viewpoint that supports you in your life, and that stops you from unnecessarily scaring yourself.

You are free now as an adult to develop peace of mind and a supportive relationship with yourself. A self-championing stance can transform your existence from struggling survival to a fulfilling sense of thriving.

You can begin right now by inviting your instincts of self-compassion and self-protection to awaken and bloom in your life.

Cognitive healing may have begun or been reinforced by reading what has preceded this. Hopefully you are having some epiphanies about what is at the core of your suffering.

Some readers may have been searching for cognitive answers for years, and through their reading and therapy already created a sizable foundation for doing this work.

At the same time, those who have only tried a Cognitive-Behavioral Approach [CBT] to healing their trauma may feel great resistance to hearing that cognitive work is important. If you are like me, you may have been introduced to it in a way that promised more than could be delivered. Cognitive tools are irreplaceable in healing cognitive issues, but they do not address all the levels of our wounding. They are especially limited in addressing emotional issues, as we will see below.

In early recovery, the psychoeducation piece of cognitive work typically comes from the wisdom of others: teachers, writers, friends and therapists who are more informed on this subject than we are. When psychoeducation reaches its most powerful level of effectiveness, however, it begins to morph into mindfulness.

MINDFULNESS

Psychologically speaking, **mindfulness** is taking undistracted time to become fully aware of your thoughts and feelings so that you can have more choice in how you respond to them. Do I really agree with this thought, or have I been pressured into believing it? How do I want to respond to this feeling — distract myself from it, repress it, express it or just feel it until it changes into something else?

Mindfulness is a perspective that weds your capacity for self-observation with your instinct of self-compassion. It is therefore your ability to observe yourself from an objective and self-accepting viewpoint. It is a key function of a healthily developed ego and is sometimes described as the **observing ego** or the **witnessing self**.

Mindfulness is a perspective of benign curiosity about all of your inner experience. Recovery is enhanced immeasurably by developing this helpful process of introspection. As it becomes more developed, mindfulness can be used to recognize and dis-identify from beliefs and viewpoints that you acquired from your traumatizing family.

I cannot overstate the importance of becoming aware of your inner self-commentary. With enough practice, mindfulness eventually awakens your fighting spirit to resist the abusive refrains from your childhood, and to replace them with thoughts that are self-supportive. Mindfulness also helps you to establish a perspective from which you can assess and guide your own efforts of recovering.

Finally, it is important to note that mindfulness tends to develop and expand in a progressive manner to all levels of our experience, cognitive, emotional, physical and relational. Mindfulness is essential for guiding us at every level of recovering, and we will examine this principle more closely throughout the book.

EMOTIONAL HEALING

Traumatizing parents do as much damage to our emotional natures as they do to our thinking processes. Consequently, there is a great deal of recovery work that needs to be done on this level. This is especially true because of the damage our wider society also does to our emotional natures.

Recovering The Emotional Nature

This section is an updated version of an article I wrote in 1991. I originally wrote it as a prelude to my first book, **The Tao of Fully Feeling**, and it was written as an appeal to the general public to understand the consequences of trying to sanitize one's emotions. Thankfully, the response I received encouraged me to complete that familial and societal damage meted out on children's emotional life.

The survivor, who is seeking a healthy relationship with his emotional being, will strive to accept the existential fact that the human feeling nature is often contradictory and frequently vacillates between opposite polarities of feeling experiences. It is quite normal for feelings to change unpredictably along continuums that stretch between a variety of emotional polarities. As such, it is especially human and healthy to have shifts of mood between such extremes as happy and sad, enthused and depressed, loving and angry, trusting and suspicious, brave and afraid, and forgiving and blaming.

Unfortunately, in this culture only the "positive" polarity of any emotional experience is approved or allowed. This can cause such an avoidance of the "negative" polarity, that at least two different painful conditions result.

In the first, the person injures and exhausts himself in compulsive attempts to avoid a disavowed feeling, and actually becomes more stuck in it. This is like the archetypal clown whose frantic efforts to free himself from a piece of fly paper, leave him more immobilized and entangled.

In the second, repression of one end of the emotional continuum often leads to a repression of the whole continuum, and the person becomes emotionally deadened. The baby of emotional vitality is thrown out with the bathwater of some unacceptable feeling.

A reluctance to participate in such a fundamental realm of the human experience results in much unnecessary loss. For just as without night there is no day, without work there is no play, without hunger there is no satiation, without fear there is no courage, without tears there is no joy, and without anger, there is no real love.

Most people, who choose or are coerced into only identifying with "positive" feelings, usually wind up in an emotionally lifeless middle ground – bland, deadened, and dissociated in an unemotional "no-man's-land."

Moreover, when a person tries to hold onto a preferred feeling for longer than its actual tenure, she often appears as unnatural and phony as ersatz grass or plastic flowers. If instead, she learns to surrender willingly to the normal human experience that good feelings always ebb and flow, she will eventually be graced with a growing ability to renew herself in the vital waters of emotional flexibility.

The repression of the so-called negative polarities of emotion causes much unnecessary pain, as well as the loss of many essential aspects of the feeling nature. In fact, much of the plethora of loneliness, alienation, and addictive distraction that plagues modern industrial societies is a result of people being taught and forced to reject, pathologize or punish so many of their own and others' normal feeling states.

Nowhere, not in the deepest recesses of the self, or in the presence of his closest friends, is the average person allowed to have and explore any number of normal emotional states. Anger, depression, envy, sadness, fear, distrust, etc., are all as normal a part of life as bread and flowers and streets. Yet, they have become ubiquitously avoided and shameful human experiences.

How tragic this is, for all of these emotions have enormously important and healthy functions in a wholly integrated psyche.

One dimension where this is most true is in the arena of healthy self-protection. For without access to our uncomfortable or painful feelings, we are deprived of the most fundamental part of our ability to notice when something is unfair, abusive, or neglectful in our environments.

Those who cannot feel their sadness often do not know when they are being unfairly excluded, and those who cannot feel their normal angry or fearful responses to abuse, are often in danger of putting up with it without protest.

Perhaps never before has humankind been so alienated from so many of its normal feeling states, as it is in the twenty-first century. Never before have so many human beings been so emotionally deadened and impoverished.

The disease of emotional emaciation is epidemic. Its effects on health are often euphemistically labeled as stress, and like the emotions, stress is often treated like some unwanted waste that must be removed.

Until all of the emotions are accepted indiscriminately (and acceptance does not imply license to dump emotions irresponsibly or abusively), there can be no wholeness, no real sense of well being, and no solid sense of self esteem. Thus, while it may be fairly easy to like yourself when feelings of love or happiness or serenity are present, deeper psychological health is seen only when you can maintain a posture of self-love and self-respect in the times of emotional hurt that accompany life's inevitable contingencies of loss, loneliness, confusion, uncontrollable unfairness, and accidental mistake.

The human feeling experience, much like the weather, is often unpredictably changeable. No "positive" feeling can be induced to persist as a permanent experience, no matter what Cognitive-Behavioral Therapy tells us. As disappointing as this may be, as much as we might like to deny it, as much as it causes each of us ongoing life frustration, and as much as we were raised and continue to be reinforced for trying to control and pick our feelings, they are still by definition of the human condition, largely outside the province of our wills.

EMOTIONAL INTELLIGENCE

Daniel Goleman defines emotional intelligence as our ability to successfully recognize and manage our own feelings and to healthily respond to the feelings of others. As implied above, I believe the quality of our emotional intelligence is reflected in the degree to which we accept all of our feelings without automatically dissociating from them or expressing them in a way that hurts ourselves or others. When we are emotionally intelligent we also extend this acceptance to our intimates. One of my clients calls this the hallmark of "relationships."

Another way of saying this is that I have self-esteem to the degree that I keep my heart open to myself in all my emotional states. And, I have intimacy when my friend and I offer this type of emotional acceptance to each other. Once again, this does not condone destructive expressions of anger which are, of course, counterproductive to trust and intimacy

Cptsd-engendering parents often hypocritically attack their children's emotional expression in a bi-modal way. This occurs when the child is both abused for emoting and is, at the same time, abused by her caretaker's toxic emotional expression.

Most traumatizing parents are especially contemptuous towards the child's expression of emotional pain. This contempt then forces the child's all-important capacity for healthy grieving into developmental arrest.

One archetypal example of this is seen in the parent who hurts his child to the point of tears, and then has the nerve to say: "Stop crying or I'll give you something to cry about!" A client once told me that he often fantasized about giving his father this angry reply: "What are you talking about, you already gave me something to cry about?!" He did not, however, because he had long since learned that getting angry back was a capital crime that would elicit the most savage retaliation. Typically it would be delivered with homicidal rage: "I'll knock you from here to Kingdom come!"

The above is of course a blatant example of the slaughtering of emotional expression. Just as common is the insidious, passive-aggressive assault on emoting which is seen in the parent who shuns her child for expressing his feelings. This is seen in the emotionally abandoning parent who sequesters the child in a timeout for crying, or routinely retreats from the crying child into her room.

The worst, most damaging example of this occurs when this is done to the pre-verbal toddler [or baby!] who only has emotions with which to express herself. Pre-verbal children are by definition far too young to learn the 2-3 year-olds' developmental task of using her words to communicate about her feelings.

An especially nasty form of emotional abuse occurs in the traumatizing family when the child is even attacked for displays of pleasant emotion. As I write this I flashback to scenes of my mother sneering at my little sister and snarling: "What are you so happy about!", and my father's frequent: "What are you laughing at – wipe that smile off your face!

Emotional abuse is also almost always also accompanied by emotional abandonment, which can most simply be described as a relentless lack of parental warmth and love. Sometimes this is most poignantly described as not being liked by your parents, which belies the many Cptsd-inducing parents who say they love their children, but demonstrate in a thousand ways that they do not like them. "The sight of you makes me sick" was very popular with such parents when I was growing up.

It can still bring tears to my eyes to remember my emotionally abandoned young sister secreted in a corner of the house begging our family dog: "Like me, Ginger, Like me!"

Chapter 6: Who Gets Ptsd?

Many people face life threatening, even terrifying events during their lifetime, but do not develop PTSD. So who get PTSD? Many soldiers during wartimes face identical conditions in which their life is in jeopardy, but not all of those soldiers develop PTSD. Why the discrepancy in the expression of this condition?

Many studies have been conducted to try and answer the above questions. Most of the conclusions reached by investigators point to one unifying fact, and that is

those who been a witness to violence, or have been a victim of violence have a stronger predisposition to the development of PTSD later in life, when once again placed in a terrifying situation.

Family Violence

Trauma from family violence can predispose an individual to PTSD.

However, being exposed to a traumatic experience does not automatically indicate someone will develop PTSD. It has been shown that intrusive memories, such as flashbacks, nightmares, and the memories themselves are greater contributors to the biological and psychological dimensions of PTSD than the event itself. These intrusive memories are mainly characterized by sensory episodes, rather than thoughts.

People with PTSD have intrusive re-experiences of traumatic events that lack awareness of context and time. These episodes aggravate and maintain PTSD symptoms, since the individual re-experiences trauma as if it were happening in the present moment.

Clinical findings indicate that a failure to provide adequate treatment to children after they suffer a traumatic experience, depending on their vulnerability and the severity of the trauma are more susceptible to PTSD symptoms in adulthood.

Genetics

There is evidence that susceptibility to PTSD has a hereditary link. It has been approximated that as much as 30% of the expression of PTSD is caused from genetics alone:

* For twin pairs exposed to combat in Vietnam, having a monozygotic (identical) twin with PTSD was associated with an increased risk of the co-twin's having PTSD compared to twins that were dizygotic (non-identical twins).

* There is also evidence that those with a genetically smaller hippocampus are more likely to develop PTSD following a traumatic event.

* Research has also found that PTSD shares many genetic influences common to other psychiatric disorders. Panic and generalized anxiety disorders and PTSD share 60% of the same genetic variance.

* Gamma-aminobutyric acid (GABA) is the major inhibitory neurotransmitter in the brain. A recent study reported a genetic variation of GABA may predispose an individual to PTSD.

* PTSD is a psychiatric disorder that requires an environmental event that individuals may have varied responses to, so gene-environment studies tend to be the most indicative of their effect on the probability of PTSD than studies of the main effect of a particular gene.

Genome-wide association study (GWAS) offers an opportunity to identify novel risk variants for PTSD that will in turn inform our understanding of the etiology of the disorder. Early results indicate the feasibility and potential power of GWAS to identify biomarkers for anxiety-related behaviors that suggest a future of PTSD. These studies will lead to the discovery of novel loci for the susceptibility and symptomatology of anxiety disorders including PTSD.

Risk Factors

Most people (more than half) will experience at least one traumatizing event in their lifetime. Men are more likely to experience a traumatic event, but women are more likely to experience the kind of high impact traumatic event that can lead to PTSD, such as interpersonal violence and sexual assault. Only a minority of people who are traumatized will develop PTSD, but they are more likely to be women.

The average risk of developing PTSD after trauma is around 8% for men, while for women it is just over 20%. The risk is believed to be higher in young urban populations (24%): 13% for men and 30% for women. Rates of PTSD are higher in combat veterans than other men, with a rate estimated at up to 20% for veterans returning from Iraq and Afghanistan.

Posttraumatic stress reactions have not been studied as well in children and adolescents as adults. The rate of PTSD may be lower in children than adults, but in the absence of therapy, symptoms may continue for decades. One estimate suggests that the proportion of children and adolescents having PTSD in a non-war torn population in a developed country may be 1% compared to 1.5% to 3% of adults, and much lower below the age of 10 years.

Predictor models have consistently found that childhood trauma, chronic adversity, and familial stressors increase risk for PTSD as well as risk for biological markers of risk for PTSD after a traumatic event in adulthood. Traumatic experiences in children is a predictive indicator of the development of PTSD later in life. This effect of childhood trauma, which is not well-understood, may be a marker for both traumatic experiences and attachment problems. Proximity to, duration of, and severity of the trauma also make an impact, and **interpersonal**

traumas cause more problems than impersonal ones.

Quasi-experimental studies have demonstrated a relationship between intrusive thoughts and intentional control responses such that suppression increases the frequency of unwanted intrusive thoughts. These results suggest that suppression of intrusive thoughts may be important in the development and maintenance of PTSD.

Military Experience

A U.S. Long-Range Reconnaissance Patrol team leader in Vietnam, 1968.

Researchers Schnurr, Lunney, and Sengupta **identified risk factors** for the development of PTSD in Vietnam veterans. The subjects were 68 women and 414 men of whom 88 were white, 63 black, 80 Hispanic, 90 Native Hawaiian, and 93 Japanese American. Among their findings were:

Hispanic ethnicity, coming from an unstable family, being punished severely during childhood, childhood anti-social behavior, and depression as pre-military factors.

War-zone exposure, depression as military factors

Recent stressful life events, post-war trauma, and depression as post-military factors

They also identified certain **protective factors**, such as:

Japanese-American ethnicity, high school degree or college education, older age at entry to war, higher socioeconomic status, and a more positive paternal relationship as pre-military protective factors

Social support at homecoming and current social support as post-military factors. Other research also indicates the protective effects of social support in averting PTSD or facilitating recovery if it develops.

Researchers Glass and Jones found early intervention to be a critical preventive measure.

PTSD symptoms can follow any serious psychological trauma, such as exposure to combat, accidents, torture, disasters, criminal assault and exposure to atrocities or to the sequel of such extraordinary events. **Prisoners of war** exposed to harsh treatment are particularly prone to develop PTSD. In their acute presentation these symptoms, which include subsets of a large variety of affective, cognitive, perceptional, emotional and behavioral responses which are relatively normal responses to gross psychological trauma. If persistent, however, they develop a life of their own and may be maintained by inadvertent reinforcement. Early intervention and later avoidance of positive reinforcement (which may be subtle) for such symptoms is a critical preventive measure.

Studies have shown that those prepared for the potential of a traumatic experience are more prepared to deal with the stress of a traumatic experience and therefore less likely to develop PTSD.

Chapter 7: Diagnosis

Post-Traumatic Stress Disorder is diagnosed by your medical care provider through the compilation and analysis of your symptoms based on your verbalized and recorded testament as well as their professional medical opinion. An addition to the diagnosis will sometimes be the presence of any previous medical or mental problems that may not have affected the PTSD directly but pose a possibility at making the treatment process slower or more difficult.

In order to have an official PTSD diagnosis, the American Psychiatric Association will require that you meet criteria based on those listed in the Diagnostic and Statistical Manual of Mental Disorders (DSM). Meeting the criteria listed will get you an official diagnosis for PTSD and allow insurance companies to take on full costs of treatment.

DSM Criteria:

The DSM as a required tool for the diagnosis of PTSD states that the traumatic event you are claiming to have occurred must have happened in the following ways:

A traumatic event was directly experienced.

A traumatic event was witnessed first-hand.

You have found out that someone close to you such a as a relative or a close friend has experienced or been present for a traumatic event.

Your job requires to be constantly in contact with traumatic events (soldier, news reporter, paramedic, fire fighter, police officer)

Required Symptoms by the DSM:

The traumatic event is constantly relived through memories, or disturbing images and thoughts that cannot be controlled.

The occurrence of dreams becomes difficult and disturbing.

The traumatic event revisits you in the form of lucid flashbacks where in you feel as though it is happening all over again.

When the traumatic event is triggered you feel emotionally weakened and physically strained.

Post Traumatic Event DSM Requirements:

You make the strongest attempt at avoiding people, places, and situations that might remind you of the traumatic event.

Remembering the traumatic event comes in bits or snippets. It is cut up and not whole.

You have become pessimistic and see negativity in yourself and in everyone around you.

Recreational activities and hobbies no longer seem appealing even if they were formerly found to be very enjoyable.

You are easily irritated and have irrational bouts of rage followed by the feeling of being numb and emotionally devoid.

You give in to behavior that may be destructive or dangerous. This may include self-mutilation, doing risky activities, or activities where you might get caught.

The feeling of being constantly on edge and watching out for things, people, or situations that might cause you harm.

Difficulty in falling asleep and staying asleep.

Remember that DSM will look for one or some of these symptoms but not necessarily all of them.

Symptoms for Children under 6 inclusions:

Using the traumatic occurrence as a means to pay. Re-enacting scenes and often displaying violence or age inappropriate behavior to playmates.

Re-occurring nightmares.

Chapter 8: Massage For Ptsd

Massage therapy is an excellent way to help manage the symptoms of PTSD. The overall goal of massage "is to help the client to become safely "embodied within the self." Massage therapists can teach clients safe and effective ways of self-soothing and stress management. People who have been traumatized are no longer at home in their bodies. Talk therapy alone does not always adequately address the fear and mistrust that has been encoded into their bodies." lvii

It is likely that you will encounter clients who are undiagnosed, but who still suffer from some form of PTSD. Women are twice as likely to develop PTSD, and since "75 percent of massage therapy clients are women,4 and given that a large majority come into massage therapy treatment for what is generally described as "stress," the percentage of clients presenting with PTSD may likely be much higher" than what you expect. lviii

Some clients will display symptoms that look more like depression than PTSD. It is important to keep a list of trusted medical practitioners to whom you can refer clients who seem to need help that is outside your realm of expertise.

Along with providing general relaxation and stress relief, massage therapy can help integrate the client's sense of body. In traditional psychotherapy, the unpleasant memories get re-encoded from traumatic memory into narrative memory. In other words, people learn to use their left brains (cortex) to coordinate their right-brained feelings. This prevents the discharge of stress hormone from the amygdala. Once talk therapy has helped the client establish some degree of narrative memory and experience of safety, clients may face intrusive body sensations with a massage therapist. Massage therapy can help clients to reframe their experience of trauma from a kinesthetic perspective." lix

Resistance From the Client

Clients with PTSD may actually prove problematic in massage therapy. They will have difficulty relaxing because of the levels of stress hormones being released at all times. They are always hyper-vigilant, paying attention to everything going on around them, which can manifest in resistance to your attempts to relax them. "In the ordinary course of events, massage therapy

can offer a profound sense of peace to those who are able to feel strong enough at their core to let go and relax. For those who carry the effects of trauma, however, the world does not feel safe and they cannot trust their bodies to give the appropriate signals of safety. Alarm bells are always being rung by the flood of stress hormones. They either remain on full alert or alternate between numbness and hyper-vigilance." lx

For clients who have experienced sexual or domestic abuse, being disrobed on a massage table can cause flashbacks, high stress and anxiety levels, as well as emotional distress. Sometimes the memories are buried, so the client does not know why they are having the reaction they are having:

"Touch of any kind may trigger memories of both desired and unwanted information. Ways that a client manages to live with the memory of a traumatic event is simply not to think about it, to deny its existence, or, at the very least, never to allow herself to consciously dwell on the horrible event.

The client may not think too much about what really happened, yet is plagued by extraordinary levels of tension. The touch of the therapist may open the floodgates of sensation which she had carefully kept closed, in order to avoid reliving the traumatic memory. If traumatic memory, stored in the amygdala of the limbic system, is triggered, then flashbacks, speechless terror, numbing, hyper-arousal and/or disassociation may result. Witnessing this may be alarming and frightening to therapists who do not expect such occurrences or who are unaware of the signs and symptoms of PTSD."lxi

The Treatment Plan

It is essential that a massage therapist be able to articulate a treatment plan to a client with PTSD in order to foster a trusting and safe relationship. Any sense of insecurity in the treatment will only worsen a client's inability to relax in therapy.

The overall treatment plan should have a defined beginning, "exploratory" mid-phase, and concluding phase. These stages can be identified as "Safety, Remembrance and Mourning, and Reconnection."

Safety, or Beginning Phase

"The initial stage of massage therapy treatment may take anywhere from one month to several months before the client feels genuinely safe in the treatment room. Emphasis at this stage of the treatment plan is on offering choices and establishing ways of contracting the ways in which the client wishes to be massaged. When she feels confident enough and ready for whatever sensory and emotional material may surface, the client generally expresses a wish to explore sensation in parts of her body that have previously not been touched, or have been either hypersensitive or numb during the massage." lxii

Remembrance and Mourning, or Middle Phase

"The middle phase can be intense, sometimes emotionally painful, and often liberating as the client receives validation from her body that she has not made all of it up, and that she can experience her body as it really is in the here and now without being overwhelmed by sensations that originate in the past. It is extremely important to note that it is not the massage therapist's role to analyze or interpret what the client is saying or feeling. In massage therapy, clients may be very vulnerable to accepting the massage therapist's interpretations as literal truth. It is always the client's right to define for herself what she is experiencing. The massage therapist must remain in the role of compassionate witness, and never suggest to clients any literal explanations of their sensations, musings, and experiences."[lxiii]

Reconnection, or Final Phase

"As treatment shifts to the final phase, the therapist begins to notice subtle changes in the client's reactions to being touched. The client may begin talking about simple and inconsequential topics during the massage-such as what she is planning to have for dinner-that do not relate to the treatment.

While she is being touched, she may talk about the ordinary events of her life and yet remain relaxed and present. There are no more ghosts of negative forces, people, and events who hurt her in the past in the treatment room. In the final phase, the client reviews what has happened over the course of therapy, embraces whatever changes the massage therapy has given, taking her learning out of the treatment room and into everyday life-a life that is now more enhanced by the possibilities of a more embodied self. For many clients, the massage therapist is a surrogate caregiver, a stand-in for those who did not or could not protect her in the past. There is often a parent-child quality to the relationship. As with all children, there comes a time when they must leave the nest and fly on their own. In many ways, the safe, boundaried intimacy achieved with the massage therapist is simply practice for clients in order to enhance their capacity to go back out into the real world, and develop new and more satisfying relationships with friends and family." lxiv

The Treatment Session

Massage therapy sessions should have a predictable and recognizable beginning, middle, and end when dealing with PTSD clients. Predictability and routine can be very comforting to patients with high anxiety levels. Tell the client what to expect at each stage of the session.

"Beginnings and endings should have familiar, repetitious aspects that signal to the client where they are in the treatment hour. The beginning of the treatment hour establishes safety, boundaries, and goals for the day. The middle part of the treatment hour is primarily experiential, and builds on the client's capacity to sustain safe touch. The ending of the clinic hour provides an opportunity for the client to articulate some of what has occurred during the treatment hour, to acknowledge what may need to be processed in her psychotherapy, and to take home strategies for healthy self-care and self- soothing." lxv

Techniques

There is no specific technique that is better suited to working with PTSD clients than another. Anything from deep tissue massage to aromatherapy, Reiki, cranial sacral therapy, and even just holding tense areas of the body have all been found to be effective. Each client's individual needs and situation will dictate which techniques are best suited for him or her. lxvi

Polarity Therapy

Polarity therapy is a good option for clients who don't want to disrobe. "Polarity therapy is based on the idea that a person's health and well-being are determined by the natural flow of energy through the body. Polarity refers to the positive and negative charges of the body's electromagnetic energy field. Practitioners use touch, movement, and other methods to help this energy flow."lxvii

"The patient lies on a massage table while the therapist scans for imbalances and checks energy flow in the body. The polarity therapist may use a variety of techniques to balance and clear energy field paths. Some of these include twisting the torso, spinal realignment, curling toes, rocking motions, and moving the hands or crystals along the body's natural energy pathways. Some techniques are similar to those used by chiropractors.

Other aspects of polarity therapy may include supportive counseling, deep-breathing exercises, diet changes, hydrotherapy, stretching, and yoga." lxviii

"This type of touch is used in Polarity to bring about awareness of one's resistance to letting go of the tension, pain and fear stored in the tissues as a result of trauma. Ms. Sullivan states, "When you touch a place that has held trauma for a long time, the psyche responds by remembering scenarios that have brought on the pain." With the re-emergence of memories associated with the trauma, the client may feel uncomfortable with touch in that area. It is imperative to respect the client's process and wishes and move on to related reflex areas."lxix

Myofascial Release

This is another technique that doesn't require disrobing, so it can be useful for relieving specific areas of tension for PTSD clients. It initiates release "of the fascial tissue restrictions held in the body from the trauma" and "Release of the emotional origin of the physical holding patterns."

"As a skilled therapist holds and unwinds these tissue tensions, memories begin to surface and release, causing the body to spontaneously "replay" body movements that are associated with the memory of the trauma. As the body relaxes and fascial restrictions release, the nervous system takes over and releases stored tensions like the uncoiling of a spring, allowing trapped nerves to elongate and restore normal function. Repressed memories are brought to conscious awareness allowing the client to look at them in a new way and experience the choice to transform them." lxx

The Studio and Environment

Your massage studio must be relaxing, quiet, and soothing, especially when dealing with clients with PTSD. If your building is a high-traffic one, try scheduling PTSD clients in the quietest part of the day. Be prepared to work without any music, or with it at barely noticeable levels. Use no scents, or very faint ones that are only designed to enhance relaxation (like lavender).lxxi

Foster a feeling of acceptance by allowing the client to disrobe to his or her comfort level, and be prepared for the possibility that the client may not disrobe at all. Try using heavier-than-usual linens for your drapings as more substantial weight can be comforting to PTSD clients.

To further enhance an environment of trust, suggest the use of a quiet signal the client can use to indicate he wants to stop, skip a specific modality or skip a body part. This can be as simple as a thumbs down. Be flexible- the client may decide in the middle of the session that he is no longer comfortable with modalities you already covered in the intake interview.

You must be willing to work with the client's reaction to the therapy.

Conclusion

The truth is bad things happen to all people at some point in their lives. When trauma hits, the real tragedy is when a person succumbs to the pain of the experience more than he or she should. When they can't seem to cope with their problems on their own, they need someone to step in and help them out.

Problems and tragedies don't always ruin people's lives, but PTSD does—unless you do something about it. A supportive friend or family member who knows when it exists, and what to do about it, is the very miracle that every single person who has the disorder needs.

While you will eventually need the help of an expert, you don't need to be a scientist to be able to help steer a person with PTSD towards the right direction. You simply have to be someone who cares.

Helping a person get out of PTSD is like saving a person from what could otherwise be a ruined life—one that isn't lived at all. It's no different from actually saving a life.

www.ingramcontent.com/pod-product-compliance
Lightning Source LLC
LaVergne TN
LVHW011955070526
838202LV00054B/4929